GETTING INTO

Counselling

JEFF RILEY

TROTMAN

Getting into Counselling
This first edition published 2001
by Trotman and Company Ltd
2 The Green, Richmond, Surrey TW9 1PL

© Trotman and Company Limited 2001

British Library Cataloguing in Publication Data
A catalogue record for this book is available from the
British Library.

ISBN 0 85660 697 9

Typeset by Mac Style, Scarborough, N. Yorkshire
Printed and bound in Great Britain
by Creative Print & Design (Wales) Ltd

CONTENTS

Foreword, Ian Jamieson, Deputy Chief Executive, British Association
for Counselling and Psychotherapy   v

Introduction   **1**
Some key terms   3

1 Counselling and psychotherapy approaches   **4**
Counselling and psychotherapy distinctions   4
Approaches to counselling   5
Analytical/Psychodynamic   5
Behavioural and Cognitive   7
Humanistic   9
Transpersonal   12
Integrative   15

2 The qualities and skills of counsellors   **16**
Self-development   16
Qualities   18
Skills   19

3 Training   **21**
Why training?   21
Who trains?   21
Choosing a course   23
More factors in choosing a course   26
Accrediting bodies   30

4 Qualifications 36

Introductory, certificate and foundation courses 36

Diploma courses 36

Advanced, postgraduate diplomas and MAs 37

5 Getting on to courses 39

Maximising your chances 40

6 Working as a counsellor 44

Counselling in medical settings 48

Counselling in the workplace 52

Looking for work 57

Salaries 57

7 Life Coaching 58

The work of life coaches 58

Coaching as a career 59

Training 59

The International Coaching Federation 60

Training organisations in the UK 61

Coaching and counselling distinctions 66

8 Further information 68

Addresses 68

Volunteering 69

Publications 70

FOREWORD

The clear benefits of counselling and psychotherapy are becoming increasingly well documented and researched. In the past year alone, we have seen the publication of Professor Michael King's £500,000 study into depression, King et al, 2000, 'Randomised controlled trial of non-directive counselling, cognitive-behaviour therapy and usual general practitioner care in the management of depression as well as mixed anxiety and depression in primary care', showing that talking treatment is the best for the majority of sufferers. We also had the publication of the massive McLeod report into workplace counselling, 'Counselling in the Workplace: The Facts. A Systemic Study of the Research Evidence', showing that therapy can reduce the symptoms of negative stress in the workplace by up to 50 per cent and reduce levels of sickness/absence rates by up to 60 per cent.

Additionally, the Mellor-Clark report into primary care, 'Counselling in Primary Care in the Context of the NHS Quality Agenda: The Facts', has demonstrated that a majority of GP practices in Britain now offer talking therapy, in addition to routine medical treatments. Between 1992 and 1998, the provision for counselling in primary care grew from 31 per cent to 51 per cent of all GP practices. Problems of a psychosocial nature now comprise the second largest presenting symptom cluster in primary care. A recent MORI poll showed that 86 per cent of the public would prefer to receive talking treatments rather than tranquillisers.

Taking these facts into account, it is no surprise that many more people are finding that they derive benefit from sharing problems with a professional listener. The general mood towards counselling and therapy seems to be shifting from one of caution to one of open acceptance. As a result, I think it is an exciting time to be involved in the profession.

Precise definitions of what counselling consists of are always controversial. It is hoped that this book will assist the public to a greater understanding. From a BACP perspective, our practitioners aim to provide clients with an opportunity to ventilate issues of concern in their lives, whether this is pent-up emotional material from the past, or a current need to evaluate and solve specific life problems.

The work is not always easy, in the sense that counsellors open themselves up to the full experience of their clients, which can be potentially distressing. However, good training enables a therapist to be able to deal with these effects in a positive way, ensuring that the result contributes to the therapeutic purpose rather than damaging it. Over time, it is hoped that therapists will find they enjoy a real sense of fulfilment too. A career in counselling can be a very rewarding experience as clients who arrive in difficulty and anguish learn how to disentangle their problems. It will probably not lead to cash riches, of course, but people are looking for rewards of many different kinds.

Some counsellors were themselves patients who have developed a desire to help others in similar distress. Others want a working lifestyle that seeks to emphasise the value of human relationships. There are in fact many different opportunities and choices open to those looking for a career in counselling – from working with bereaved clients, through helping couples or family groups with behavioural problems, to providing support for those suffering from redundancy or unemployment. Some therapists choose to specialise in given areas like rape counselling or trauma therapy, eating disorders or pastoral care. Many of our members work in the Health Service and voluntary organisations; increasing numbers work in large companies; many prefer private practice.

The number of people giving and receiving counselling and psychotherapy in the UK continues to grow. The membership of the British Association for Counselling and Psychotherapy itself has expanded from about 6000 in 1992 to almost 20,000 trained, registered and supervised therapists today. Our message to the public seeking therapy would be – Why look for a practitioner outside one of the large regulating organisations like BACP?

Our offices in Rugby, Warwickshire, receive in excess of 2000 requests a month for the names of counsellors in a specified area. There is a similar number of requests for information on training to become a counsellor. At BACP, we always encourage members to work towards accreditation in a move aimed at standards throughout our profession. Whether you decide to become a counsellor or not, most people enjoy the training, which tends to includes an element of personal development and increased self-awareness that can be a delightful experience in itself.

As I said earlier, it is an exciting time to get involved in the profession.

Ian Jamieson, Deputy Chief Executive, BACP

Careers-Portal
the Online Careers Service

Careers-Portal has the most comprehensive information on careers and higher education on the web

- Facts and figures on all kinds of careers
- HE: Uncovered
- Over 2000 links to universities, job & careers sites
- Art & Design – the guide to winning the HE place you want
- £3000 up for grabs in our 'Win Your Rent' competition
- And lots more...

So come online and see for yourself the advertising potential!

www.careers-portal.co.uk

INTRODUCTION

The counselling and therapy movement is becoming pervasive. Up to half a million people in Britain regularly use counsellors. For example, teachers under stress working in a failing school may phone a counselling service provided by their trade union; members of the emergency services traumatised after a major disaster routinely have counsellors to help them recover; record numbers of sufferers of seasonally affective disorder (SAD) are now seeing counsellors. Around 50 per cent of GP surgeries (up from 30 per cent in 1992) now provide access to counsellors to help with illnesses such as depression, phobias, food disorders and impotence. Others may visit their regular counsellor as routinely as they go to the gym or stay in hotels, where an on-call therapist is now just part of the service.

The growth in counselling is also being driven by the fact that counselling skills are now recognised as a valid part of many different professions and roles. Counselling courses, for example, regularly attract managers, human resource professionals, social workers, nurses and doctors. It is estimated that over 2.5 million people use counselling skills as a major part of their jobs. There are also large numbers of people working and training in a voluntary capacity as counsellors for organisations such as Relate (marriage guidance), Mind (mental health) and Cruse (bereavement), reflecting another aspect of the burgeoning counselling scene – the development of specialised areas.

There are over 400 different types of therapy available, and a ballooning number of training courses for potential counsellors and therapists to choose from, an increase from 76 training organisations in 1990 to over 540 today. This rapid expansion is also indicated by the annual growth in membership of the British Association for Counselling and Psychotherapy (BACP) and the fact that there are now around 300,000 counsellors in the UK (compared to 30,000 junior doctors). This growth

1

has been accompanied by a mixed press. Recent controversies have included Recovered Memory Therapy, which led many ordinary people to believe, falsely, that they had been sexually abused as children. One professor of analytical psychology has described psychotherapy as 'a profoundly risky business with an irreducible shadowy aspect' while others have described it as 'remunerated handholding' by 'merchants of hope'. This suspicion is nevertheless giving way to the arguments *for* therapy, not just through numerous surveys that regularly show consumer satisfaction but through evidence from scientific research. While it is true that many of the benefits of counselling are incapable of scientific proof ('you can't do a double-blind trial on the efficacy of a three-year course of analysis') evidence now exists that shows the benefits of various forms of psychotherapy in a range of psychological debilities such as depression, schizophrenia and personality disorder. One recent study, cited by the therapist Susie Orbach and presented to the Royal College of Psychiatrists annual conference, demonstrated that people were benefiting from physiological as well as psychological changes after only six sessions.

Controversy surrounds the movement partly because it is not fully established nor as regulated as a profession. While many practitioners are registered voluntarily with one of the two main psychotherapy organisations there are countless unregistered therapists. There are, in fact, no legal qualifications for those working in the field. Privately sponsored but government supported proposals in the House of Lords to regulate psychotherapy have recently failed. These would have controlled entry into the profession via accredited training organisations (scrutinised by larger 'umbrella' bodies) and mandatory registration. Nevertheless the government has indicated that it wishes to see further regulation. The main psychotherapy bodies are also strongly in favour and have put in place many measures that will facilitate it in the medium term.

This drive for professionalisation has been controversial within the counselling and therapy movement. There are counsellors and counselling organisations concerned that the development is introducing an inappropriate medicine-type 'consultant culture', driven by a trade association response to a saturated market rather than concern about 'protecting the public'. Despite these debates there is a broad consensus about the value and importance of training.

You are probably reading this book because you are considering counselling and are rightly, given the time, expense and sheer dedication involved, concerned to choose the most appropriate route and training course. Whether you are intending to change your career, augment your skills for your present role or are considering some counselling training for purely personal development this book will show you how to go about it.

The book also includes a chapter on life coaching (Chapter 7). This is an increasingly well-known role in the UK that draws on some of the same skills as counsellors, though clearly differentiated from counselling in terms of the rigour of its training and its career paths.

SOME KEY TERMS

Many different professionals are involved in the counselling field. It will be useful to broadly distinguish the main groups:

- **Psychiatrists** are medical doctors who have taken further training in psychiatry. It is a specialism alongside others such as surgery, general practice and paediatrics. Psychiatrists diagnose and treat people with clinical mental illnesses such as schizophrenia.
- **Psychologists** are concerned with human behaviour. On its own the title has little meaning, but Chartered Psychologists usually have a degree in psychology (postgraduate conversion courses are available) and have undergone further qualifications and supervised training to enable them to practise psychology without supervision. Psychologists treat people suffering from psychological distress that includes a wide range of conditions, from addictive behaviours to anxiety. The professional body is the British Psychological Society (BPS).
- **Chartered Counselling Psychologists** are Chartered Psychologists who are members of the BPS's Division of Counselling Psychology and have specialised in counselling psychology.
- **Chartered Clinical Psychologists** are Chartered Psychologists who usually work in medical or mental health settings and may have additional specialisms such as child clinical psychology. Their clients are likely to be suffering from acute mental illness such as phobia, panic attacks and obsessive disorders. This book, however, focuses on **counselling** and **psychotherapy**.

3

Chapter 1
COUNSELLING AND PSYCHOTHERAPY APPROACHES

Confusion can surround the distinctions between these processes. Some commentators see no essential differences between them and use the terms interchangeably and some may flippantly see the difference as about status ('about £8000 a year'). Others see counselling as a humanistic branch of psychotherapy. It will be useful to start with some broad distinctions often drawn between these key terms and define some other important concepts we will come across.

COUNSELLING AND PSYCHOTHERAPY DISTINCTIONS

- Psychotherapy is aimed at helping people understand the underlying cause of their severe and persistent difficulties and come to terms with their problems. It is a long-term process. Counsellors usually help clients to focus on particular problems at an immediate level and approach specific difficulties. It has a short-term focus.
- Psychotherapy focuses on personality change while counselling helps individuals utilise their own coping resources. This has been seen as a distinction between 'revolutionary' and 'evolutionary' change.
- Psychotherapy work often centres on talking about patients' feelings and thoughts about childhood and early relationships. The issue of transference and the unconscious world of patients are involved and their past life re-experienced in the present. Counsellors by contrast work with the here and now and the focus is primarily on the conscious material provided by the client.

- Psychotherapy practice is rooted in psychodynamic theory while counselling is underpinned by the theories developed by humanistic writers such as Carl Rogers.
- Psychotherapy courses usually require either a relevant degree such as psychology, relevant qualifications in related areas such as social work, nursing or indeed counselling, or possibly relevant life experience such as work in human resources. Counselling courses have no specific academic entry requirements.

APPROACHES TO COUNSELLING

Theory is an important factor contributing to the effectiveness of counsellors and therapists. However, there is much less orthodoxy available in the field than in many allied disciplines. There are hundreds of different therapies and at least 12 major underpinning theoretical approaches. Different courses reflect these different and sometimes antagonistic emphases. On the other hand many training courses will have modules that introduce students to the range of distinctive traditions, traditions which, in many cases are influenced by or evolved from one another. However, training is a major investment in time and money. Potential trainees will need to be familiar with the main theoretical traditions informing modern counselling practice and consider which of them will suit their own personality and ideas.

ANALYTICAL/PSYCHODYNAMIC

Psychodynamic counselling developed out of psychoanalysis, the therapy founded by Sigmund Freud. From early in his career Freud was interested in the notion that psychological disorders might have their source in the mind rather than the brain. He noted how, under hypnosis, some physical symptoms, such as the paralysis of a limb, disappeared, emphasising the power of mental states of which patients were not conscious. Freud developed a thesis which suggested that much mental activity is unconscious and that emotional disorders are caused by repressed traumatic memories of childhood. These were uncovered through techniques such as free association, the interpretation of dreams, thoughts and feelings emerging through reveries on the couch and noting slips of the tongue ('Freudian slips'), misreadings and the forgetting of names. Once revealed, repressed or forgotten aspects of the psyche can be reconciled with the patient's conscious life. Freud's theories and methods drew around him many gifted analysts who developed his ideas, some of which became distinct enough to lead to the founding of separate schools of analysis and psychotherapy.

The school of analytical psychology, for example, is derived from the work of Carl Jung. Jung accepted the importance of bringing individual unconscious motivations and feelings to the conscious but also postulated the existence of a 'collective unconscious' that contained a common biological and social history. The unconscious could contain positive things and even things that have not yet happened. The analytical psychologist (also known as a Jungian analyst) will try to understand unconscious elements in what the patient says and the dreams they report. Jungian analysts believe that everyone is able to heal themselves and enrich their lives. While analytical psychologists treat people with emotional disorders or problems with relationships they also work with 'normal' people who are looking for a better balance or sense of direction in their lives.

While psychoanalytic theory and practice continue to evolve psychodynamic counselling courses will cover the theories of these and other founding analysts and are founded on some basic assumptions:

- The psyche contains both unconscious and conscious elements.
- The unconscious largely determines behaviour. Through analysis it is possible to understand one's unconscious and gain insight into memories of traumatic events that are hidden and which have been affecting our conscious lives.
- Events can affect our lives in different ways depending on the developmental stage at which they occur.

Traditionally psychoanalysis involved patients seeing their analyst five times a week over several years. Patients lie on a couch with the analyst in a chair behind their head and are encouraged to say whatever comes into their consciousness. As adapted in psychodynamic counselling it is a less intense activity and represents less of a time (and financial) commitment for patients. Though the couch may still be used patients usually sit facing the therapist for one to three sessions a week.

Freud would still recognise many of the techniques used by psychodynamic counsellors. For example, they listen and interpret to help their patients and themselves understand what is underlying the patients' responses, while telling the patient very little about themselves. Freud felt that, in the absence of information about the therapist, patients are enabled to experience or re-experience important early relationships, particularly with their parents, by transferring these on to the analyst. This phenomenon of 'transference' was facilitated by the use of the couch and subsequent lack of eye contact, which helped to present patients with more of a blank screen on which to project. Contemporary psychodynamic counsellors continue to work with transference; for example, patients may unconsciously be equating their therapist negatively with a punishing father or positively with an affirming father ('both an illusion', as one therapist said).

The relationship between counsellor and client is complex and transference can also be introduced by the therapist into the equation. This is one reason why psychodynamic counsellors are expected to have psychoanalytic psychotherapy themselves. Counsellors need to be aware of their own transference patterns and the way in which they may be affecting their relationship with their client.

Clients may come to a psychodynamic counsellor to help them deal with a recent crisis or difficult emotional experience but often the work becomes developmental and an opportunity to address more global issues and review core values. The approach is intellectually demanding and will suit those who want to work over a longer period of time with their clients. The psychodynamic approach has also been developed to facilitate work with groups, in brief therapy settings and in family counselling.

BEHAVIOURAL AND COGNITIVE

Behavioural

Freud's psychology centred on the interplay between the unconscious and conscious mind. For FB Skinner and his mentor JB Watson, central figures in the development of the theories underpinning the behavioural approaches to counselling, behaviour is determined not by the decisions of an inner self but learnt through stimulus response associations. Behavioural habits are learnt and repeated until they become automatic. However, what is learnt can be unlearnt and behaviour that causes distress can be replaced by good ways of behaving. Responses can be positively reinforced by pleasurable consequences and negatively reinforced by unpleasant outcomes. For example, schoolchildren can learn to behave well if their good behaviour is reinforced by praise and rewards and bad behaviour leads to their being ignored.

These and other principles of behaviourism, such as the belief that apparently complex behaviour is actually a collection of simpler elements understood in terms of basic learning principles, have been developed into therapeutic methods by therapists such as Wolpe. Using the behavioural technique of desensitisation, for example, enables specific irrational fears (phobias) such as claustrophobia, agoraphobia and the fear of flying to be overcome. The therapist will obtain information about the feared object or situation through the patient's verbal responses, diagnostic tests and even interviews with friends or family members. A step-by-step method takes patients through hierarchies of fear-provoking stimuli, until the fear abates. The behavioural method is typified by the focus on a clear goal achieved by rewarded practice often approached through the taking of small steps.

The techniques of behavioural counselling are intended to be non-punishing. Punishment would only suppress the expression of responses, not eliminate them. There is an element of teaching involved as patients learn useful patterns of behaviour. Interactions between clients and therapist are centred on structured action plans geared towards specific aspects of the patients' life and the achievement of tangible goals.

Cognitive

The introduction of cognitive theory has widened the breadth of work of behavioural counsellors since the late 1970s. This approach addresses a person's mental processes, perceptions and assumptions – their cognition or 'internal philosophy' – as well as their behaviour. In other words the construction people put on a particular situation affects their emotional and behavioural reaction to it. For example, three people fail the same accountancy exam. One may be angry because they expected to pass easily; another becomes depressed because they feel they have become worthless; while the third may be glad because they didn't really want to become an accountant. Cognitive theory is founded on the notion that human beings are not simply shaped by their environment but have a wide range of responses available to them. We are able to reflect on our behaviour, observe others and regulate our responses based on our thoughts. The approach helps clients by identifying and modifying thoughts that are leading to maladaptive behaviour. The therapist and client develop safe and manageable routes that allow negative automatic thoughts to be recognised and alternatives suggested.

Cognitive theory is widely used in the NHS to deal with anxiety problems such as obsessive compulsive disorders (excessive hand washing for example), panic disorders, depression and relationship problems. Cognitive training has also been used to help the long-term unemployed move into work by improving their self-image. It is usually brief work (up to 20 sessions) with follow-up sessions to check progress and reinforce the relearning.

A distinctive variant, rational emotive behaviour counselling (REBC) was founded by Albert Ellis in 1962. His basic premise was that people seek to achieve basic goals such as survival, freedom from pain and happiness. Our personal philosophies may serve us in our aims or undermine us. REBC counsellors help clients dispute irrational beliefs and reshape their personal philosophies. Therapy can take the form of 30-minute sessions over six weeks to deal with a specific symptom or, for more thoroughgoing change, last six months or more. REBC counsellors have to engage with the underlying philosophical frameworks their clients use and have a direct and challenging approach to irrational beliefs. The emphasis on rational belief means that REBC is not generally used for clients who are very disturbed or who have only a slight hold on reality.

HUMANISTIC

The premise of the humanistic approach is that people are motivated by a uniquely human need and capacity to take power over their own lives and realise their potential. This process of self-actualisation can help human beings solve their own problems and heal their own psychological hurts. However, the right conditions for self-actualisation have to exist. The therapist's role is to help provide the conditions for clients to explore their own experiences, strengthen their self-concept and innate tendency to self-actualisation. The approach has been seen as a useful corrective to the medical model based on assumptions of illness, symptoms and emotional neutrality. Key humanistic approaches include the following.

Person centred

This approach, pioneered by Carl Rogers after the Second World War, is person centred because the helping relationship activates a self-healing process located within the clients themselves ('the client knows best'). The quality of the relationship between client and counsellor is crucial. A complete absence of threat is required and the therapist provides the basic or 'core' helping conditions of genuineness, empathy and unconditional positive regard. While the existence of unconscious factors is acknowledged by Rogers they appear less as a disturbing source of instinctual energy than 'taproots' to the true self.

The emphasis on providing a supportive relationship requires the person-centred counsellor to be non-directive and to engage at a personal and direct level with what clients present.

Gestalt

Gestalt was founded as a therapy by Fritz and Laura Perls in the 1950s and was further developed by Paul Goodman and others. The theory postulates that people have the innate capacity to interact creatively with their environment in the furtherance of their perceived needs, to satisfy hunger, to take a simple example. This requires a number of things – an awareness of the need, mobilisation (action) on the part of the person (say going to the fridge and getting something out), and the availability of the fridge (that is, the support of the environment). Deviation from this balance (homeostasis) signals the need. The need may, of course be emotional, such as the need for comfort. There may also be deviations from homeostasis because the person is experiencing too much, so the need is, say, to use the loo (to continue with the 'hunger' cycle) – or to withdraw from contact for some quiet time.

Gestalts are the cycles of awareness and contact that form the satisfaction of needs. The therapy looks at the interruptions (or neurotic processes) that prevent the completion of Gestalts.

The therapist's job is to help the client become aware of these interruptive processes and, by so doing, to allow change to happen. It is understood that these processes were developed by the person as a creative response to the prevailing situation in early life but have continued into adult life where they have become counter-productive. By exploration of the original meaning and purpose of the interruption and also by gaining appreciation of the present situation and its new supports and constraints the person is freed to interact more successfully with their world.

Techniques used include the empty chair, which allows clients to express feelings that in the original situation they could not – thus completing unfinished business. The inner conflict between present need and neurotic interruption can also be explored using two-chair work, leading to a reordering of the imperatives of the client's inner world.

While Gestalt has the reputation of being confrontational, a present-day practitioner will be trained to recognise the level of support/challenge appropriate to the particular client in front of them.

Transactional Analysis (TA)

Eric Berne, who first developed TA, acknowledged Freud's structural model but focused on those aspects of the structure available to conscious awareness. He defined three ego states of the personality – Child, Parent and Adult. The 'Child' contains those spontaneous ways of seeing and engaging with the world that we bring from our childhoods. The 'Parent' holds our individual social rules derived from parents and other parent figures. The 'Adult' is our rational analysis of reality. Being in different ego states can influence our behaviour and relationships and the ego states continually interact, conflict and inform each other in creative and destructive ways.

In transactions the ego states all have a part to play and may result in communications that are clear, conflicting or hidden, or mixed (ulterior transactions). TA looks at life scripts developed in childhood – the automatic patterns of expectations learnt from childhood may have become unhelpful, for example leading us to play games or have rule-bound communications at the expense of fulfilment and self-realisation.

TA theory recognises four possible life positions in attitudes to other people:

- I'm OK, You're OK' – reflecting a healthy acceptance of self and others.
- I'm OK, You're not OK' – a defensive 'racket' that shows a sharp division between the sources of good and bad experience.
- I'm not OK, You're OK – a depressive perspective rooted in the childhood experience of relative powerlessness compared to adults.
- I'm not OK, You're not OK' – a position of despair reflecting a view of the world as fundamentally untrustworthy.

TA therapists work with clients towards the 'I'm OK, You're OK' position by looking at their transactions, the life scripts they use and the limiting pay-offs they receive from game-playing communications. Through enabling their clients to access their spontaneity and ability to abandon rule-bound behaviours the TA therapist helps them to become less fearful of intimacy and more self-aware. The therapist has a contractual relationship with the client with clarity about goals and what the client wants to change and works as an educator or parent to help the client replace the 'Not OK' scripts.

TA has application in counselling and, because of its emphasis on communication, is also applicable in training, management, education and other areas where understanding people is central. The four fields of application (specialities) are: Clinical (Psychotherapy), Counselling, Organisational and Educational.

TRANSPERSONAL

The transpersonal is the fourth of the major divisions of counselling and psychotherapy practice. Transpersonal implies 'that which is beyond the personal', in other words that which connects, unites and transcends us but which is experienced individually. The word itself is said to have been coined by Jung. He, along with early pioneers such as Assagioli, spent many years researching and exploring ways in which the human experience included a desire for something beyond the material world. Nevertheless it is the most recent approach to have established itself in the field. Transpersonal approaches:

- Postulate the existence of a spiritual centre of identity, the Self, that includes the personal but goes beyond it.
- Accept that spiritual drives and urges take their place alongside basic psychological ones. For optimum health the higher needs for self-realisation must be met. The goal is to help the client meet their range of needs – physical, emotional, mental and spiritual – according to their individual temperament.
- Suggest that individual lives benefit from identifying a meaningful and fulfilling purpose.
- Recast crises and pain as points and opportunities for growth and recognise that they are connected with an individual's drive for self-realisation.

Transpersonal therapists will use distinct techniques in addition to those common to psychotherapy, such as visualisation, dream work, journalling or the use of meditation. Clients may be asked to draw or sculpt a feeling or experience, enabling expression in non-verbal modes. Physical disciplines and work with the body can be used to integrate the body, mind and spirit. Ceremonies and rituals have their place in helping, both evoking and containing the energies of transformation.

Psychosynthesis

The founder of psychosynthesis, Roberto Assagioli, trained as an analyst but felt that Freud had labelled man's higher values and achievements as adaptations of basic instincts and drives. For Assagioli higher impulses, desires and motives exist in their own right. Our present is affected not just by our psychological past and the conditioning brought about in childhood but also by our psychological future or the vast human potential for healing and change. Repression of this higher potential can lead to psychological disturbance in the same debilitating way as the repression of childhood trauma. Psychosynthesis therapists are concerned to deal with both sources of disturbance but seek to guide clients to understand the meaning of their human life. Key concepts in the theory include:

- **Exploration of the unconscious.** Contact established with the inner universe of feelings, memories and images, including aspects of ourselves relegated to the unconscious because they are too painful or conflict with the conscious image we have of ourselves. The inner world contains various personalities and sub-personalities – 'impulses, desires, principles and aspirations are in continuous tumult'.
- **The I.** Self-knowledge leads us to understand that there is a danger we may identify with and become enslaved by a single facet of ourselves, such as anxiety, fear, prejudice, neediness or even the party goer. Thus we become dominated by an illusion. We become centred by consciously detaching ourselves from the aspects of our personality.
- **The will.** The awareness of our true centre is a decisive step forward. However, to avoid the recrudescence of old complexes there is a need to discover and use the will. This is not a Victorian repressive phenomenon but a cluster of responses including something instant, such as an act of courage or the making of an irrevocable decision; or it may be that time when we focus and persevere with a project such as writing a book! These moments and patterns of choice and decisiveness reveal the existence within us of will.
- **Superconscious.** Just as there is a lower unconscious so there is a superconscious. In this realm we may experience the transcendental, moments of epiphany, an outpouring of creativity and glimpses of a sense of unity with all beings.
- **Human beings desire to act freely** in accordance with their own intrinsic nature. However, there is a complementary urge to harmony, to feel part of a larger whole; to enter into relations with others, transcending the limits of individuality, and express friendship, tenderness and love. A healthy person will recognise and develop the ability to express both needs.
- **Synthesis.** The essence of psychosynthesis is the harmonious integration of all or component parts around a unifying centre. The grand purpose as expressed by one of the psychosynthesis institutes is

'the unique expression of individual life within a larger evolutionary context of humanity's destiny on earth'.

INTEGRATIVE

Integrative therapy is best considered by those who have already received a grounding in one of the prior, major models. It recognises significant connections between many different therapies that may be unrecognised by their exclusive proponents. It is respectful to each approach but draws from many sources because it believes that no one approach has all the truth.

Chapter 2
THE QUALITIES AND SKILLS OF COUNSELLORS

SELF-DEVELOPMENT

Most counsellors will have had some positive experience of therapeutic help in their own lives that acts as an inspiration for their counselling practice. It is, in any case, a mandatory element in most training courses. Beyond this, however, the work itself requires a *continuous* process of self-development that is complementary to, but goes beyond, the notion of a state of self-awareness. The old proverb 'physician heal thyself' is adapted in counselling to 'counsellor know thyself'.

People usually go to see counsellors because they are in state of crisis and distress. One patient used a metaphor of a cruise ship in dry dock for repair to describe his therapy. The patient felt the therapist was having to be concerned not with his presented positive self, what he saw as his elegant ballrooms, polished brass and varnished floors but, instead, was having to deal with the unpleasant stuff that is normally hidden from the world – below, as it were, the waterline. These were the destructive encrustations of barnacles and weeds that were his neuroses, repressed memories, shame, anger and fear. To be with clients in this part of themselves and create a safe place for them to think the unthinkable and say the unsayable demands that you yourself have been prepared to face your own hurts and uncertainties.

Amongst the issues that need to be addressed as starting points for self-awareness before embarking on training are the following.

Motives for helping

You will undoubtedly be asked about your motives for embarking on counselling training. It is essential that you are able to grow to understand how the work will serve your own needs and aspirations. Having clarity about your motives will help you to ensure that they do not distort the therapeutic relationship; for example, a commonly expressed motive for students in training is that they 'want to help others'. This is helpful in so far as it expresses an unselfish concern and can buttress the endeavour of the counsellor to offer warmth and to value clients. However, the motive can become problematic if it expresses a need to be seen as the 'good person'. A counsellor may, for example, end up wanting people to be happy so much that they actually inhibit them from expressing and exploring their unhappiness. To take another example – where emotional pain may be the source of motives. If you have gained strength from dealing with your own past traumatic events you may be able offer more sensitivity to others exploring their own trauma. However you may, on the other hand, be suffering from unresolved emotional pain and unconsciously be using clients to deal with that rather than helping them.

Feelings

How do you react when confronted by the expression of feelings? On a counselling course you may meet feelings through listening to someone talk about their feelings; witnessing someone expressing feelings through crying or being angry; dealing with your own feelings that arise. To be able to help someone counsellors need to make sure they are aware of potential emotional blind spots of their own. Peter Sanders in his book, *First Steps in Counselling*, quotes Carl Rogers:

> 'If I can form a helping relationship to myself – if I can be sensitively aware of and acceptant towards my own feelings – then the likelihood is so great that I can form a helping relationship toward another.'

Counsellors will have to address other issues about themselves during their training, issues about their values and ethics; about their class and race attitudes; their sexuality and their sense of worth amongst others. Exploring these can be both exciting and frightening.

QUALITIES

As we have seen different theoretical approaches are based on different theories of the personality and, furthermore, these approaches may suit people's different individual styles. Nevertheless there are certain qualities common to the work of good counsellors. These include tolerance, stability, warmth, patience, intuition and sensitivity. We look now at how some of these qualities are utilised by counsellors.

Empathy

This is the ability to sense the patient's world as if it were your own, with an emphasis on the 'as if' element. This was one of Carl Rogers' core conditions but is now given emphasis across many therapeutic approaches. There are two aspects involved. The first is the ability to comprehend a person or situation and to allow our awareness to be acted on; to be in touch, for example, with a client's depression or bereavement. The 'as if' aspect, however, emphasises the second aspect, a separateness. The counsellor is not at that moment depressed or bereaved and this contributes to their ability to listen, observe, reflect and explain.

Personal maturity

Counsellors will know that there are times when clients will perceive them through previous experiences. One therapist has described sessions in which clients have 'given them a pasting'. On the other hand there are moments when clients' history will make them see the counsellor as a very kind, wise or loving figure. This kind of response is known as transference and a counsellor needs to be able to respond without being 'seduced' or becoming defensive. The determination to explore the origins of these feelings has to take priority. This means counsellors being prepared to be on the end of strong feelings of hate, fear and anger. This requires a high level of personal maturity and stability.

Acceptance

This quality can also be described as non-judgmental warmth. Rogers called it unconditional positive regard. It does not imply that counsellors have to approve of their clients' behaviour or 'love' them but the helper must be able to believe that the client is fundamentally worthy and hold them as a human being of equal value.

Training courses will help students uncover what they find shocking or disgusting and perhaps extend their range of tolerance. Nevertheless as a counsellor you may find yourself struggling with feelings aroused by supporting someone who, for example, is a convicted rapist or who has a political stance that you find unacceptable. However, it is also the case that the actual struggle for understanding can play its part in the therapeutic process.

SKILLS

In addition to such qualities counsellors will need a range of specific skills. These may be learnt and practised and will feature on training courses. Some of the basic skills include the following.

Paying attention

This goes beyond the notion of simply active listening. It means attending to the whole range of signals radiating from a person: words and sounds certainly, but also non-verbal signals. What about the person's voice quality? For example, is it soft, hard, confident or weak? Is somebody's breathing deep, shallow or relaxed? Is the facial expression happy, fearful, relaxed? The counsellor has to gather and interpret clues about the person and pay attention to help understand the client's thoughts, feelings and behaviour. By suspending judgement about the client and setting aside our own experiences and feelings we are enabled to communicate empathy and respond sensitively.

Reflection, paraphrasing and clarifying

To understand the meanings of the client counsellors will employ reflection and paraphrasing and will clarify.

■ **Reflection** involves, at its most basic, echoing back the content of what has been said, in essence saying to the patient, 'I am listening carefully to what you are saying and trying to understand. I heard what was said. Did I get it right?'

- **Paraphrasing** involves summarising what the client has said. This may involve using the client's words or your own. Training courses will help you build up your vocabulary around feelings.

- **Clarifying** does not mean imperiously summing up the client's feelings from a position that implies you see more sense in their world than they can. Rather it enables the counsellor to obtain clarity about their understanding of the client's world. At the same time this will communicate to the client that you are trying to understand and help the client gain clarity by encouraging them to explain in more detail.

Developing a trusting relationship

There are certain practicalities that will allow you to create a safe place for clients to explore their issues. These include clarity and consistency around day, time and length of sessions and the provision of a counselling room that is discrete and comfortable. However, the relationship is also developed by verbal and non-verbal communication that indicates warmth, genuineness, empathy and acceptance. Counsellors will be trained in techniques that help them hold their clients as intrinsically worthy, to keep that valuation separate from the client's behaviour and to enable them to transmit this position in the therapeutic process.

These techniques include being specific in communication and avoiding generalisation. For example a counsellor might say, 'It sounds as if losing your job was a heavy blow for you', but not 'Redundancy gets everybody down at first'. The latter response may be intended as comforting but could be read as 'your loss is no different from many others and your pain and fear are unnecessary'.

There are many other skills and qualities that counsellors have to draw on in their practice. Not least are intellectual and conceptual capacities that will enable you to work at a postgraduate level. You will have to thoroughly understand, interpret and apply complex theoretical models. Many counsellors have to apply their skills while incorporating the demands of specific employers and particular settings.

Chapter 3
TRAINING

WHY TRAINING?

Most people go to see counsellors and therapists because they are undergoing a crisis. They expect that the person from whom they seek help will offer an appropriate mix of theoretical knowledge, a level of skill and practice in working with clients that has been supervised and a personal maturity and suitability. A training course should provide an opportunity to explore all of these elements in increasing depth and complexity.

While there are currently no legal qualifications for those working in the field there is an increasing amount of self-regulation and it is likely that some form of statutory requirements will be introduced by the government for those therapists working within the NHS. This tendency will mean that significant areas of counselling and therapy work will only be available to those who have undergone appropriate training courses. For example, the Association of Child Psychotherapists is recognised by the Department of Health as the body that accredits UK training in child and adolescent psychotherapy.

WHO TRAINS?

Training in itself is a period of change and crisis for those undertaking it. It is also a long and usually expensive process. For these and all the above reasons those wishing to train will need to choose their training organisation and course with a great deal of care. This may not be a straightforward exercise. One recent web site endeavouring to put together a list of counselling courses was lobbied by institutions requesting a listing – 'the first college wanted to list courses such as "Art of Nature and Self-development through Shamanic traditions" and the second college wanted to list a "Free Meditation Course"'.

Training institutions can be broadly divided into three main types, discussed below.

Universities and colleges

Counselling courses are available at a range of academic levels on a part-time or full-time basis. Colleges and higher education institutions offer everything from introductory and taster courses through Higher National Diploma (HND) courses and on to first degrees, Masters and Phd-level qualifications. This sector has been a traditional source of training for psychologists and for members of associated professions such as medicine, social work and nursing. These have increasingly recognised the value of counselling in their work and the sector developed courses initially to support this training. Now a broad range of qualifications cover many different theoretical approaches suitable for a wide spread of employment areas.

Courses offered in academic institutions, particularly at postgraduate level, may be approved by or working towards approval by either the BACP or the United Kingdom Council for Psychotherapy (UKCP). In addition they will have to meet the standards required by the government's Quality Assurance Agency. Entry qualifications may be academic such as A-levels or vocational A-levels, but institutions are usually able to consider relevant previous experience. While counselling courses are found across the range of levels, psychotherapy courses are postgraduate and will require either a degree or equivalent-level studies or experience.

As well as an emphasis on academic content courses will offer the opportunity to develop practical counselling and therapy skills through placements and group exercises. HND and undergraduate courses will have briefer placements than more advanced courses that are aiming at meeting the requirements of the BACP and UKCP. The lower-level courses will not require students to participate in or offer personal counselling or therapy.

In recent years academic institutions have increasingly validated courses run by other training organisations, which means that students can obtain degrees and postgraduate qualifications by studying outside the university sector.

Psychotherapeutic and psychoanalytical training organisations

There are a large number of specialised organisations offering a range of counselling and psychotherapy courses. Often they will have been developed to promulgate a particular therapeutic approach. More recently institutions and courses have been able to adapt their theory and practice to incorporate other therapeutic approaches including counselling. This development means the student may be able to choose from institutions that focus on a specific approach or consider those which offering a more integrative approach covering several models. It is becoming increasingly important that institutions and courses are recognised by accrediting and umbrella bodies such as the BACP, the UKCP or the smaller British Confederation of Psychotherapists (BCP).

Voluntary organisations

These are organisations such as Alcohol Concern, Cruse Bereavement Care and Relate, which offer care and support in the community on a range of issues. Counselling training is available for volunteers in the organisations ranging from National Vocational Qualifications (NVQs) to MAs. While the experience and qualifications gained through involvement with such organisations can be useful for those seeking a career in counselling they may not be recognised by the professional bodies.

CHOOSING A COURSE

As part of the process of choosing a course you will need to consider a number of questions, for example:

- *What is my motivation to train and work in this way?* This will undoubtedly come up during the selection process. You will need to have some clarity about your motivations to avoid disappointing yourself and potentially damaging your clients.

- *Which approach will suit me?* As we saw in Chapter 1, different theoretical models will suit different personalities.
- *Which training am I eligible for?* It would be a useful starting point to consider any training you have already undertaken. Perhaps you have already taken some courses with a counselling element. Perhaps you have studied subjects that have some relevance, such as education or child studies. Have you undertaken relevant scientific research? In addition do you have any relevant experience that uses counselling type skills? For example have you worked in a voluntary organisation? And have you undergone any personal therapy or personal development work? What kind of theories underpinned the type of therapy you have taken?

Courses will be looking for a combination of qualities, academic abilities and qualifications. Institutions will be concerned that you are a stable personality and may not be able to consider you if you are in need of medication or have a serious psychotic condition. Courses also have minimum age limits, with 25 being a typical point at diploma level. Foundation or degree-level courses may well have lower age limits.

- *How much time will I need?* Different types of training will demand different amounts of time. Training as a volunteer may not cost you money (though that may well change) and will take less time than a BACP- or UKCP-approved course. On these courses it may be worth noting what one institution advises about its trainings – while 'trainings are part time in terms of contact hours, the Diploma and MA should be considered a full-time commitment which will have a major impact on the trainee's life at many levels'. However, courses are available in many different formats and some may be geared to fit well around a full-time job or other commitments.

One foundation year course at the Institute of Psychosynthesis comprises the following elements:

1 orientation day in September
9 weekends
1 week summer school
8 x two-hour study groups
10 x two-hour large group forum
40 therapy sessions
6 written assignments

However, as courses progress you will find that they make increasing demands on your time. At diploma level and above the course will have to be made your number one priority, particularly as by that stage you will be expected to have started seeing your own clients – at least two a week. You will also be required to undertake client supervision. This might be done in groups with other students but often requires students to engage their own supervisor for additional exploration of their practice. You will also be seeing your own therapist, a mandatory element on psychotherapy courses and on most counselling courses. This will involve between an average of one to three sessions a week, with counselling courses demanding less than psychotherapy routes. You will need time also for reading and this could average around three hours a week. Courses have a significant theoretical input and demand an appropriate amount of reading and time for researching and writing essays, often at a demanding postgraduate standard.

■ *How much money will I need?* Of course training involves an investment of money as well as time. Course costs are made up of a number of elements, including some that may not be obvious, so watch out for hidden extras such as supervision costs and the costs of your own therapy. One diploma course has the following cost breakdown:

Registration fee	£25
Insurance	£35 (to protect you and clients in case of injury or claims of professional negligence)
Admin fee	£35
Course fee	£1480
Supervision fees	(included)
Cost of own therapy	£2520 – 72 hours at £35 per hour
Total	**£4095**

These are *annual* charges and this particular course lasts three years. Some course fees do not include the cost of supervision, which then has to be paid for separately.

MORE FACTORS IN CHOOSING A COURSE

Before deciding on your training course make sure you are clear about the following:

- **Course content.** What core theoretical model is being used and what are the options for studying other models?
- **Quality assurance.** Who validates the qualifications? Who are the training staff and what are their qualifications? Some, for example may hold BACP Accredited Trainer status. Are the trainers likely to be able to teach you in the areas of your interest?
- **Framework.** How big will the classes be and what tutorial support is there? The staff/student ratio will make a difference. Too few students will mean you may have a less varied input and too many may make it difficult for you to get individual attention. Consider also how big the groups are and whether group sizes will be comfortable for you to contribute to. What is the library like? Is there a complaints procedure and how are your views taken into account – is there a trainee association, for example?
- **Training methods.** Courses should have a large element of practical and experiential or 'hands-on' learning. There are distance learning or correspondence courses available at certificate level and some, but not all, include some practical training days. These courses may be suitable as an introduction, particularly for those who for reasons such as disability are unable to attend mainstream institutions, but ideally face-to-face training is preferable. You should avoid distance learning advanced courses at diploma level and above, not least because they are unsuitable for those seeking courses recognised by mainstream accreditation bodies.
- **Clients and placements.** How much help is given in finding a placement? Is there a placement officer and a list of potential placements? Does the training institution have clients it may refer to you? Some organisations will be able to provide a professional reception and referral service and even provide the facilities for you to see clients in.
- **Academic work.** Courses will require you to complete assignments to demonstrate what you have learnt. It might be worth finding out from the beginning exactly what will be required and when. For example,

are your written essays expected at the end of the course or are there deadlines to meet throughout? And exactly how long do the essays have to be? A course may require, say, three essays of 2500 words in a single year or one 4000-word essay. Essays are only one form of assessment. The following are the formal assessment items for a part-time counselling diploma at the University of East London:

Year one
Personal transition paper (2000 words approximately)
Multicultural/Social context case study (2000 words approximately)
Audio tape transcript and commentary
Personal journal (5000 words approximately)
Professional log (not less than 5000 words)

Year two
Psychological type essay (2000 words approximately)
Counselling practice case study (3500 words approximately)
Personal journal (5000 words approximately)
Professional log (not less than 5000 words)
The log includes records of client work, supervision, self-development, audio-visual laboratory work and feedback as well as client case notes and self-appraisals.

■ **Validation.** Note which validating bodies are involved with the organisation. The increasing amount of regulation and professionalisation involved in the field will encourage you to consider courses coming under the aegis of the key bodies in the field (the BACP, the UKCP and the BCP). Remember, however, that while some courses may be perfectly acceptable they may not have been running long enough to have gained approval from these bodies, but still subscribe to their guidelines and work within their code of ethics. You might also want to take soundings from counsellors whose opinions you trust when deciding on courses.

Many institutions encourage you to attend open evenings or short introductory courses before you enrol on a training course. They are excellent opportunities to gather information and get answers to the above questions. Open evenings may be free or carry a nominal charge. Shorter courses (which may last anything from one to five days) could cost between £100 and £250.

CASE STUDY

Training in counselling

Farah Zeb is a trainee counsellor, nearing completion of a Diploma/BA Hons in Person Centred Counselling at the Metanonia Institute. Farah came to this course for a variety of reasons.

> 'As an Asian person I had found it quite difficult to find a counsellor for myself with a similar background. I needed to explain everything that was different and important to me. Even though the counselling that I had previously received from therapists who were not from a similar ethnic background was supportive and insightful, at some level I continued to feel unmet. For me, finding someone from a similar ethnic, cultural and religious background was important.

> 'I decided to train in counselling not only to try to fill in a gap in service provision for Asian clients but also for my own personal development as an individual person and a social being. Furthermore, I wanted to validate the personal skills that I had acquired through working for a local voluntary rape crisis helpline and my full-time job working for the authority homeless persons unit. Skills that involved listening, understanding, remaining calm and unbiased, being non-judgemental, being empathic and being clear and honest about the limits of what I could realistically do.

> 'I do not, at this stage in my life, wish to set up as a sole practitioner in private practice, as I would find the financial investment very demanding and the absence of professional contact with other colleagues quite isolating.

Farah chose Metanoia only after doing some research.

> 'Firstly Metanoia had been recommended to me by someone I trusted and valued. Metanoia ran a BACP accredited training course and was convenient geographically. It also offered a part-time, modular weekend learning route that suited me in terms of being able to continue my employment and pay for the course. Furthmore, I was searching for a course that provided a learning experience which, in addition to academic requirements, would also include and value experiential understanding and worth. Metanoia did offer this alternative style of learning, which appealed to me.

28

'Initially I attended a brief open discussion on whether counselling was for me and then attended an introductory workshop, which outlined the different courses and routes available in counselling training. I felt that the counselling approach based on the work of Carl Rogers best suited my personality.

'For every individual the length of the training in terms of completion depends on their own personal process and pace, which in turn depends on life situations, changes and experience.'

This course has taken Farah several years and will be completed when she is ready to submit a case study and sit a final viva exam. After the completion of her diploma, Farah will also have the option of applying to submit some further work in order to acquire a degree in counselling.

'The course has taken me longer than I had initially expected or anticipated. Metanoia does offer accreditation of prior learning, which I did not have the confidence to negotiate about at the onset of training. In addition, much has changed for me personally in terms of my life and growth. All the time that I have needed has indeed been worth investing in. I do not feel that this is a course for anyone who is in a particualr hurry to complete it.

'In terms of what I felt the course lacked was an overall and in-depth awareness of cultural, religious and ethnic diversity that is not necessarily only eurocentric in its mindset and structure. I am told that Metanoia is trying to meet that gap, but I am aware that it remained unfilled for me.

'Even though the course itself has been quite painful and challenging, at times it has also left me feeling quite elated and free. It is a huge roller-coaster of emotions and thoughts that taps into a deeper level of personal feelings and questioning mindsets. Even though I had been in personal therapy before starting the course, the diploma really got me to look at who I was and my own way of being. I left most modules feeling quite fragile as a result of all that had come up for me. Even though during training modules there is an appropriate and boundaried space in which personal feelings arre given a voice and space, trainees are encouraged to be in personal therapy for their own additional support.

'In terms of being assessed on the training, I remember feeling quite apprehensive when one of my counselling sessions was being observed by a tutor for whom I had emormous regard. It was difficult to separate from being observed and assessed, rather than judged and criticised. To be myself with a real fellow trainee client who was bringing their own real and personal material, in a slightly unreal situation, and remain grounded was a difficult experinece. The tutor was very supportive and the experience has registered as a positive learning experience for me. Pieces of written work have also been a requirement and although reading the relevant books adds weight to the learning, I have always struggled to find enough time for it, alongside a full-time job and other responsibilities.

'I feel that the course has helped enhance my counselling skills, made me much more aware and thoughtful about my interactions with clients and with people in general. I feel that I am a much more grounded, socially open and accepting person. I feel that my relationship with myself has improved and that I have learned to listen to the wiser, inner voice of my mind, body and soul and therefore enabled a better understanding of my thoughts and feelings.'

ACCREDITING BODIES

The profession is currently regulated to an extent by the voluntary registers and rules of a number of significant bodies.

The British Association for Counselling and Psychotherapy

The premier organisation representing counsellors in the UK also has a significant number of members who work as psychotherapists. Amongst its aim are:

- maintaining and raising standards of training and practice
- providing support for counsellors and those using counselling skills, including continuing professional development
- representing and promoting counselling both in the UK and internationally.

Amongst the services it offers the counselling and psychotherapy movement are the United Kingdom Register of Counsellors (UKRC). This offers protection and information to the general public and extends professional recognition and accountability. The register includes independent counsellors and registered sponsoring organisations. In both cases registration is dependent on meeting assessed practice criteria. UKRC counsellors have to be appropriately trained and qualified and work to the BACP Code of Ethics and Practice. If necessary, members will be subject to complaints procedures.

Individual members have to be members of BACP or of the Confederation of Scottish Counselling Agencies.

BACP also has an *accreditation scheme* for individual counsellors. While accreditation is not a legal requirement, and currently most counsellors are not accredited, many people embarking on a counselling career are working towards BACP accreditation. Accreditation is a direct route to registration with the UKRC. Accreditation means accruing a set number of hours in skills development, in theory and in practice.

There are different routes to accreditation (for those working with individuals or couples – accreditation does not apply to group counselling). The two most pertinent ones for those considering counselling as a career are:

- **Completion of a BACP Accredited Counsellor Training Course** and accumulation of at least 450 hours of counselling practice supervised over not less than three and not more than five years. Approved training courses then provide an opportunity for you to build up your supervised hours of practice towards this target.
- A total of 450 hours of successfully completed counselling training comprising two elements:

  1) 200 hours of skills development and 2) 250 hours of theory . Any reasonably substantial core counselling course may be counted for accreditation purposes. This route also requires that you offer at least 450 hours of supervised counselling practice.

There are a number of other criteria that applicants have to fulfil. These include:

- an agreement for continuing supervision
- evidence of a commitment to ongoing professional and personal development
- being able to demonstrate practice that adheres to the BACP Code of Ethics and Practice for Counsellors
- a philosophy of counselling that integrates training, experience, further development and practice; evidence of at least one core theoretical model should be demonstrated
- evidence of having completed a minimum of 40 hours of personal counselling or an equivalent activity consistent with the applicant's core theoretical model
- evidence of serious commitment to working with issues of difference and equality in counselling practice.

Evidence that applicants meet these and the other criteria is presented in a written application that includes two case studies.

It is worth pointing out that this individual accreditation scheme is separate from the accreditation scheme for training courses operated by the BACP. There is no automatic route to accreditation on completion of courses. All successfully completed courses, even those not accredited by the BACP, can count towards an individual accreditation application and be assessed as part of the completed submission.

BACP course accreditation

The BACP accredits courses all over the UK. Courses are recognised as meeting certain standards. On successful completion of such courses students might reasonably expect to function as counsellors. Courses are likely to be of one year's full-time duration or two to three years part time with a notional minimum of 400 contact hours. Short courses are, therefore, not able to be accredited by the BACP. To become accredited courses must have graduated at least one cohort of students; courses have to be reassessed every five years. The validation process covers course design and its delivery and assessment processes. The rigorous process guarantees students undertaking an accredited course a number of things:

- courses contain eight basic elements: admission, staff development, client work, supervision, skills training, theory, professional development and assessment

- a grounding in a core theoretical model
- a balance between theory, skills components and personal development consistent with the core theoretical model
- assessment processes include regular, constructive feedback
- courses help students develop as reflective practitioners, who are also required to monitor and evaluate their own work and personal development
- the course should be appropriately staffed with not less than two core members for any course
- the course will include a placement with a counselling service; it is not considered appropriate for inexperienced students to gain all their client work experience through work with clients seen independently.

COSCA (formerly the Confederation of Scottish Counselling Agencies) runs a similar scheme in Scotland that also offers an opportunity to be listed in the UKRC. The COSCA accreditation system, however, is different in both process and requirements.

The United Kingdom Council for Psychotherapy

The UKCP exists to promote psychotherapy and maintain high standards in the profession throughout the UK. It maintains a National Register of Psychotherapists (separate from the BACP). The UKCP is an organisation of organisations and its members comprise the great majority of reputable psychotherapy bodies in the UK, representing all the main traditions in psychotherapy practice. Membership is voluntary and currently numbers around 80.

Joining the UKCP register of over 5000 individual members brings a number of benefits. These include recognition from the largest umbrella body for psychotherapists in the UK and publication in the national register, which is published annually. To join the register you must be in, and maintain membership of, one of the UKCP's member organisations and adhere to the UKCP-approved Code of Ethics and Practice and be accountable to the UKCP complaints and appeals procedures.

Organisations joining the UKCP usually join one of of eight sections, each representing a different approach to psychotherapy. The Council sets training requirements for all the sections. Many training institutions are members of the UKCP, offering accredited training leading directly to UKCP registration. Other member organisations may accredit training in the UK or accredit individuals with qualifications, skills and experience gained outside of the UKCP's structure.

Training requirements set down by UKCP include:

Entry requirements
Entry is at postgraduate level of competence.
Candidates must have personal qualities that make them suitable for the profession of psychotherapy.
Candidates should have relevant experience of working with people in a responsible role.

Basic requirements of training courses
The training shall be at postgraduate level.
The course shall not normally be shorter than four years part-time duration (or the equivalent).
The training will cover a minimum curriculum.

Member organisations are obliged to state whether a specific qualification coincides with recognition of candidates as eligible for registration by UKCP and, if not, what further professional development is required for registration.

British Confederation of Psychotherapists

Like the UKCP the BCP is an organisation of organisations and operates a voluntary register. It is, however, a considerably smaller organisation. The BCP register of around 1300 individual members contains separate sections for those working with adults and those trained in work with children and adolescents. Its member organisations are specifically psychoanalytic in nature. They include mostly very long-established psychoanalytic psychotherapy organisations. Some of the BCP's members have dual membership with the UKCP.

Each member organisation of the BCP has its own prerequisites and requirements for training. Minimum requirements though include a degree or qualification in medicine, psychology or social work (or equivalent) and some experience in the field of mental health. Accredited training has to be of four years in length. Trainees have to be in analysis or therapy a minimum of three times a week and undertake extensive supervised clinical experience with two approved supervisors and attend seminars covering theory and technique.

Chapter 4
QUALIFICATIONS

The complex plethora of schools, beliefs, practices and doctrines is extended to the qualifications structure the movement makes available. The anticipation of statutory registration and the shift to professionalisation is leading to a review of the qualifications framework and this will in turn lead to some streamlining. For the moment, however, the tremendous diversity and richness of courses available is accompanied by the potential for some confusion. While a definitive study of qualifications available would require a book to itself students will find many courses under the following categories.

INTRODUCTORY, CERTIFICATE AND FOUNDATION COURSES

There are many short or introductory courses ranging, for example, from a single weekend to ten evening sessions. More substantial courses may take the form of one-year, part-time courses. Usually no formal qualifications or experience are required for entry to these kinds of courses. They usually contain students who are taking them purely for self-development as well as those with ambitions to practise. These courses fall outside the ambit of accreditation by bodies such as the BACP and UKCP though the staff taking them may well be accredited trainers.

DIPLOMA COURSES

The above courses may, however, serve as access to, or be an entry requirement for, diploma courses. Diplomas may take between two and four years, full or part time. They will usually require you to be obtaining clients by the second year, if not earlier, and often a placement is also required. They are suitable for those wishing to practise professionally and they can be accredited by, for example, the BACP or UKCP. They may well also carry undergraduate degree course status or, particularly in psychotherapy training, Masters awards, as psychotherapy is considered postgraduate training.

ADVANCED, POSTGRADUATE DIPLOMAS AND MAS

These more advanced courses are often associated with those who wish to practise psychotherapy or who are aiming to practise counselling as independent practitioners. You will usually need a degree or equivalent and experience of counselling in a face-to-face context. The MA awards are a separate qualification but may also be awarded to those on diploma courses completing additional academic work. They last between one and two years.

CASE STUDY

Self-discovery as a therapist

Susan Hayes illustrates the definition of therapy as a continuous process of 'learning from the patient'. Her work as a therapist has always been an extension of a programme of self-discovery that began when she attended the Centre for Counselling and Psychotherapy Education (CCPE) as a patient. *'My therapist suggested I took the foundation course at the college as a further way of getting to know myself'*, says Susan. *'I fell into it almost without realising it but when I was on the course it felt like home.'*

Susan eventually completed the diploma course at CCPE and now usually has between four and a maximum of seven clients. She says:

'It was never my intention to set up a private practice. At the moment I have four clients, including one I have worked with since I began training in 1994. I still see a therapist myself and am interested in further training. I have participated in many weekend workshops and recently began group therapy. My UKCP membership means I have to pay for regular supervision and mandatory updating courses. So therapy isn't particularly for me a way of making money.'

Nonetheless the issue of payment is important and Susan remembers clearly the moment on the course when she accepted her first payment for a counselling session:

'I enjoy working with clients but payment introduces the notion of boundaries, setting time limits and raising the status of the session and in particular the client's sense of worth.

'It is not a game, and as I have become more confident and my own sense of self-worth has gone up I have felt able to increase my fees. It seems quite different from my early counselling work on the course as a volunteer at a hospital in the cancer ward, where I was creating a role as a befriender and support counsellor. One patient – who was very gentle with me – had throat cancer and suggested, I think seriously, that this was what I wanted to do. With another patient language differences meant we could "only" sit and hold hands. This was a big learning point for me, that I don't have to "do" anything. I'm still learning that.'

Susan combines her therapy work with her main career as a choreographer and is happy with that balance.

'I get most of my clients through referrals from CCPE and I have rarely ever advertised. In the future I want to explore more group therapy, which I love. Or maybe make my choreography work more aligned through using more body-oriented therapy. I believe whatever way I take, therapy will always be a two-way process for me.'

Chapter 5
GETTING ON TO COURSES

Counsellor training is popular and there may well be competition for places. Even introductory courses may expect to interview you. Diploma and other advanced courses will certainly require you to attend a selection process of varying length and complexity. Interviewers will be looking at a combination of factors. As we have already seen motivation is important and you will need to have an understanding of the benefits that the course and the work will have for you as well as what you hope to contribute.

Courses are not the place for sorting our your own problems. The fact that you have faced traumatic events, dealt with periods of depression and struggled to deal with phobias or addictions will not exclude you from training. You may well have learnt a lot from confronting such problems and your experience may usefully inform your practice. Selectors will, however, be concerned that you have been able to achieve a new level of stability. You will also need to show that you are able to offer a consistent time commitment not only for the course but for your clients in practice.

In addition to formal qualifications and appropriate experience applicants will need to show that they have the relevant personal qualities for practice, education and training. See Chapter 2 for details of these qualities.

Questions you may be asked include:

■ *Describe the most significant turning points in your life and what impact they had on you.*
■ *How would you describe your current support system?*
■ *What changes would you like to see in your life during the next few years? Expand on why these changes seem to be important.*
■ *Why do you want to do training at this time?*

It is not necessary to have everything about counselling or about yourself worked out – after all that is what the training is going to focus on. However, at your interview you will need to be able to demonstrate self-awareness and an ability to be thoughtful. It is better to have a period of silence, for example, while you find the correct expression than rush out a less considered answer.

If the institution incorporates group interviews and case studies as a method of selection it will still be looking at the factors mentioned above but will also be assessing how you interact in groups. It will be important that you are able to strike an appropriate balance between listening well and contributing.

MAXIMISING YOUR CHANCES

Even applicants to introductory courses may be expected to provide evidence of their use, or potential use, of counselling skills and attitudes. Many applicants may be able to demonstrate this through doing related employment such as social work, human resources or teaching, but without this kind of exposure you may need to consider doing some voluntary work to build up your experience. There are lots of volunteer organisations that work with people in crisis which need the help of committed individuals. Some, such as Relate, offer a first-class training for their volunteers that will support your application for counselling and therapy courses and help you bring important experience to your training. Other organisations such as the Samaritans and Cruse also offer an opportunity for training in and putting counselling skills to use. Volunteer counsellors need to find an organisation that offers training, an opportunity for support and supervision, appropriate premises to work from and guidelines to work within. A useful starting point to finding suitable organisations is the National Centre for Volunteering (see Chapter 8). You might also contact your local volunteer centre and check in your local library for potential organisations.

CASE STUDY

Working as a Relate counsellor

Tony is an experienced counsellor, having worked for Relate (and Marriage Guidance, its predecessor) for 20 years. He trained as a counsellor after a successful career as a corporate lawyer. He still clearly recalls the rigorous selection procedure ('*an eagle-eyed interviewer – very penetrating questions and analysis*') but obviously enjoys his vocation and recognises the value of Relate's work. He says:

> 'Relate counsellors help people in the central relationship of their lives. Couples and families can face difficult issues that can lead to major social problems. Even after 20 years it is still enormously satisfying. There's precious little money in it though!'

Since the tough selection procedure and rigorous training course Tony has continued to develop his counselling skills. He is now one of a few contract counsellors who work alongside volunteers. '*Society has changed – child abuse came much more into the public arena ten years ago and violence – domestic violence – across all races and all classes is also now more openly talked about. But we are also finding out just how much more of it is other changes, including the fact that we now see gay and lesbian couples and more couples in "blended families", families made up of children and partners from previous relationships. There are additional Relate courses to help us deal with these specialised areas.*'

Tony's experience enables him to conduct 'initial interviews' as well as dealing with the general marriage problems that form the bulk of the issues brought to Relate. He comments:

> 'The initial interview is carefully designed to gather information for the counselling sessions subsequently conducted by a colleague, though it may also serve as a stand-alone session. We establish the key facts about the family structure, the nature of the presented problem, how the couple feel about it, what has worked, if anything, and if there are any other professionals – perhaps other counsellors – already involved. As an experienced counsellor it is my job in that first hour to put this together.'

In fact many clients find this first interview sufficient. Where appropriate, clients will be referred to other agencies – '*We don't counsel for addictions,*' says Tony, 'or *psychotic mental illness – these are beyond our brief and we refer on to self-help groups or psychiatrists respectively*.'

Relate's clients are a cross section of the entire population. '*Most people from 20 to 80 years plus are potential clients*', says Tony. The range of issues couples bring is also wide:

'On the surface it could be about money or about couples not having time for each other. Our work and training are geared to getting beyond this presented problem and to help deal with the underlying issues. This could be unresolved grief or something rooted in the individuals' own history. Sometimes the surface problem can be quite intimate – for example impotence – but the underlying issue could be a material one, financial worries or bankruptcy. Whatever areas the sessions cover – and most couples on average have six to eight one-hour sessions – Relate and its counsellors do not seek to impose any particular result or set of values. When we see people who have powerful feelings for each other they may have a relationship that could, and perhaps should, continue. However, we can equally find that we are dealing with a relationship that is fatally flawed or should never have started in the first place, and we offer loss work for those who wish to part.

'Both partners need to be involved, even if one partner is more extrovert. Our psychodynamic training equips us to understand how both parties are drawing on their separate histories and at different levels bringing to bear different expectations and models to their relationship. Couples may be suffering because of their own poor parenting. They may have no viable role models or have a naive view of romance taken from TV. Whatever it is, we are dealing with people who are in pain.'

Client confidentiality is a major concern:

'If possible we use only people's first names. What we tell clients is always private unless they or another party is being harmed, or at risk of being harmed. In this case we would have to think about whether anyone else would need to know. This is particularly important where children are involved. If we consider anyone to be at risk we do warn clients that we will expect them to take responsibility and seek help or we may have to disclose the matter to the appropriate authority ourselves.'

Nationally Relate seeks clients feedback systematically and can also on occastion receive feedback locally from clients. Clients may make a special effort to express their thanks. 'We *could never initiate it,*' says Tony, '*but I will find myself approached or waved at in the street and occasionally there will be a card that will say things like "this is my baby's photo – who wouldn't have been born if we hadn't overcome our problems with your help."*'

Chapter 6
WORKING AS A COUNSELLOR

After the arduous and exciting challenge of obtaining a diploma you will be ready to develop your career as a professional counsellor. The variety of potential work areas can be partially illustrated by considering the membership divisions available to those joining the BACP. These comprise the Association for Counselling at Work; the Association for Pastoral and Spiritual Care and Counselling; the Association for University and College Counselling; Counselling in Education; Personal, Relationship and Groupwork; Race and Cultural Education in Counselling. There is also a separate Faculty of Health for those working in medical settings.

In addition to these member divisions there is also a distinction to be made between those who go on to work in an agency and those who work as independent practitioners. Many training institutions provide awards that reflect this division, with independent practitioner level set at the more advanced standard.

There are advantages to beginning your professional career in an agency. Clients are supplied by the agency that will be well known in its area. The agency will also take clinical responsibility for the counselling it provides, ensuring that responsibility for the service provided is divided between yourself, the agency counselling manager and your supervisor. Other benefits include the sense of community provided by working in a team.

Independent practioners do not always work in private practice. It is also possible to work as an independent practitioner in an agency. For example many agencies have won contracts to work in primary health care teams in general medical practice, to provide counselling services in workplaces as part of an Employee Assistance Programme and even to provide student counselling services.

The rest of this chapter will give you a flavour of the work of counsellors in some of the different settings available after training.

CASE STUDY

Independent practitioner in private practice

Having been taught by Anna Freud as a psychology student and met regularly with Donald Winnicott while deputy head of a school for severely disabled children Brian Maunder's eventual avocation as a psychodynamic psychotherapist was not, perhaps, a surprising career change.

'My qualifications (I had taken an MEd in education and psychology) and previous experience meant I was able to go straight on to the Counselling Diploma course at Westminster Pastoral Foundation (WPF) and then through to the psychodynamic psychotherapy course. The course included lots of practical advice for those who were considering private practice. So I knew even before I left that producing lots of marketing materials, advertising, and bombarding GPs' surgeries with letters would be a complete waste of time. I have built up my practice gradually through word of mouth, networking and personal contacts. I took a small group of about five clients with me who had been referred to WPF during my training. At that time I thought it desperately important to be near them geographically as I had no local contacts near where I live in south-east London. So I hired a suitable (and expensive) room in central London. Now, with more experience, I realise that clients will travel once the therapy is well established and the process of transference is under way.

'As it happens I do now write to GPs but I do it to let them know when I have one of their patients referred to me by a psychiatrist colleague. It is a courtesy letter but it is also a fairly targeted piece of marketing. To be honest building up a full-time practice is a gradual process. Without a small pension from my career in education I would have struggled to survive. People have to take on all kinds of work in their early days. Voluntary work, low-paid sessions, work in GP surgeries – anything to get their name known – and they combine it with other types of work. I was able to be discriminating and say "I can't help" and refer on when appropriate while, at the same time, keeping my sharp sense of purpose to build my practice.

'There are a lot of expenses involved in running a business. I now have dedicated rooms with a partner analyst in our house. This has involved decorating, building work (including a survey for the soundproofing, which alone cost £1000) and the provision of a separate loo. Even the furniture, decor and ambience in the rooms have to be durable, appropriate and chosen with care – patients can work with what is in the room and it isn't fair to patients to change it thoughtlessly. There are also continuing expenses such as cleaners, business rates, administration and an accountant to pay. My accountant has experience in the medical field – which is significant in surprising ways – he gets me money back on the flowers and tissues I have to buy! Quite apart from creating the right conditions for individual clients the premises will be inspected by Employee Assistance Programme type organisations such as the Independent Counselling Advisory Service before they will refer clients to you.'

Brian has built up a strong base of clients and has an average of 15 clients for between 28 and 32 sessions a week:

'That is around 1000 sessions a year. I am strict about taking holidays, however. I work for 40 weeks of the year and the remaining 12 are funded, frankly, by the increased fees I charge. As long as clients are given notice they are able to accommodate breaks. As well as holidays I think making a contribution to my professional bodies (in my case the UKCP and FPC (the Foundation for Psychotherapy and Counselling) – the graduate body of the Westminster Pastoral Foundation) is also vital – making you part of your community, and it also helps you "retemper steel". That amount of work with distressed and depressed people can be quite hard. So I attend courses, conferences and edit a newsletter. This kind of networking is also good for my practice and is an opportunity to give out my business card – I do get referrals that way.

'Like many things I have to do in private practice that kind of extrovert orientation doesn't come naturally to me. In my experience therapists tend to focus more on the "inner world", or stay close to the patients – and, in my case, just go for a walk on the hills. It is important however because it opens up other possibilities. For example, I do some supervision, I teach and I do some consultancy work. Currently I am helping London Council prepare for membership of the UKCP. I have also undertaken a selection process that enables me to act as a therapist to trainees on their courses. This kind of work adds variety to my portfolio as well as extra income. And that is also important. This is a very rewarding living in many ways but not one where you are going to make a lot of money.'

Many trainees setting out will hope eventually to develop their own independent counselling practice. Brian's case study illustrates a number of points about the challenges that will face them in their ambitions to run an independent, small business.

Firstly, as necessary in any small business, Brian has developed a quality product. His therapy training flowed from a lot experience in related fields. He also takes care to keep in touch with the profession and makes sure his skills are kept up to date. Those wishing to work as independent practitioners might consider taking advanced-level courses offered by some training institutions designed to prepare counsellors for independent practice. Those setting up in independent practice are often at the level of experience that would allow them to obtain registration as a BACP accredited counsellor.

Secondly, his product has been brought to the attention of those people most likely to need it. Brian has been able to do this through a variety of methods, combining focused marketing, networking and word of mouth. Thirdly, as his business matures Brian has made careful judgements about the fee level he has set and the hours he works, setting levels that ensure he doesn't get burnt out and leaving enough time for continued professional development and other activities. Therapists often work within ethical guidelines that include advice on the recommended number of client contact hours.

There is clarity about exactly what he is able to offer and an awareness that he may not be the most suitable person to help everyone who approaches him. Novice counsellors may be tempted to see inappropriate clients as they seek to build their practice, or to think that they can help the suicidal, psychotic or severely disturbed where the medical profession appears to have failed. One reason experienced therapists and counsellors are able to be selective about who they see is because, like Brian, they have diversified away from total dependency on the client caseload. Typically activities such as supervision, training, teaching and writing work can add income streams.

And finally, many of the skills needed to run a successful practice are not those you most immediately associate with counselling, for example control over the financial and administrative aspects of the practice. Note how Brian uses professional help from an experienced accountant. Setting up in practice can be a major investment. The consulting room has to be private and discrete and designed to be comfortable without being intimidating. Even the provision of toilet facilities needs attention – after all strong feelings will affect metabolisms. Ideally, as in Brian's case, there should be completely separate facilities, including the provision of a separate telephone line on which clients can leave confidential messages.

COUNSELLING IN MEDICAL SETTINGS

It has become increasingly recognised that counselling and psychotherapy have an important role to play in the medical context. Despite the rapid growth of sophisticated medical techniques the active participation and involvement of the patient are a vital aspect of preventive medicine and in the management of chronic illnesses. In addition more practitioners are embracing the concept of holistic medicine, which pays attention to the patient's psychological and social factors as well as physical illnesses.

Counselling skills are widely used in the sector by nurses, doctors, social workers, occupational therapists, volunteers as well as psychotherapists and counsellors.

General practice

The growth in the numbers of counsellors associated with GPs' surgeries reflects both the growing recognition of their role in medical care and that it has become easier for them to be funded. Some are funded directly by the practice they work in and others through Family Health Service Authorities.

Secondary care and hospital settings

Counselling has a role at many stages of medical treatment – from screening and preventive programmes through diagnosis and treatment, but also when no further active treatment is possible. Psychological distress is the most common reaction to illness; and relatives can be affected by distress, which again affects the patient. Distress can be reduced by providing information about the illness and treatment but this is not always a straightforward matter. Training in counselling skills is important so that the patient's understanding, what they want to hear and what they can cope with can be taken into account. Patients needing to make a decision about treatment may talk to a counsellor about the alternatives confronting them, indeed some treatments and procedures, such as HIV screening, mastectomy and abortion, may require the involvement of a counsellor. However, while a number of hospital departments have counsellors as part of their team there is no guarantee that they have counselling qualifications.

CASE STUDY

Counselling in higher education

Anna Hellmann is in charge of the counselling team at London Guildhall University. She says:

'Work in this sector is hugely popular with counsellors. There is real variety in the range of issues students bring. We're not specialised in the sense that alcohol counsellors are or as we would be if we were employed by, say, the fire service, where the same problems might crop up year after year. In any case we get a new cohort of students every year to work with alongside existing clients.'

'*I originally trained as a social worker,*' says Anna. '*I then taught social work practice in further education, which led to a role as a student services officer.*' This work involved offering students welfare advice as well as personal counselling. '*My employers at that time sent me on day release and I took a Diploma in Student Counselling at Birkbeck College*'. The course had a psychodynamic foundation based on Freud, Klein and Winnicott ('*Freud was God*', says Anna). This approach still underpins much of Anna's work:

'Winnicott, for example has much to say about the way children react to the outside world, and to understand how a person's history links to their "here and now" you have to look at the unconscious. Today I have an'"existential" element in my work, for example taking into account the impact of poverty, cultural differences and institutional issues – essential in the university setting.'

The mission of the counselling team and the Department of Student Affairs in which they are based is to help students succeed despite personal or financial problems. To do this the cultural background of the student body has to be understood.

'We are a community or "local" university, 80 per cent of our students live at home. They are not typically "lonely" or "homesick" as with some groups of students in old universities but over half of our students are from British black and Asian ethnic minority groups. Many come from non-traditional backgrounds and are first-generation university students.'

This can have a huge impact on how students cope with becoming independent learners. '*Many of our students come to us with practical problems, for example a student may find her family pressing for an arranged marriage in the middle of exams; or students may find the combination of money and study problems leading to pressure to drop out.*' There is no evidence to suggest that student problems are worse than in the general population, though some of their issues are student specific. Students will, of course, be referred to appropriate support organisations within the university for study skills, for example, but the team offers students up to 6 counselling sessions, or 12 under special circumstances.

This is very brief therapy. Anna is aware that much of the therapeutic literature recommends that brief therapy runs from 6 to 12 sessions or to six months. 'Most students only want one to six sessions', she says. '*We feel that what we offer is different, not lesser. Sterling work can be done with motivated students who are interested in personal growth and change.*' Many students in fact opt for a single session as part of a formalised 'mitigating circumstances' process and the average sessions are four per student – this figure reflects the national picture. Anna has noticed significant changes in the clients over the last decade:

'Students' circumstances and histories have grown much more complex. On the other hand British people are much readier to talk about personal issues. And such things as sexual abuse are now much more in the public arena. Overseas students are more reluctant, as they are unfamiliar with counselling and still feel there is a stigma attached to it. Students may come to see us initially for a single session because they have been unable to hand in a piece of work by a deadline. We may be able to support their claim for mitigating circumstances and for some this will lead to them looking at the story of their life for the first time.'

Those students who need longer-term psychotherapy with such problems as severe depression and anxiety are referred externally, though some trainee counsellors working from the centre may also offer an extended programme of help as part of their professional training.

Typical 'pinch points' for students during the academic year occur around exam times, academic deadlines and during the first semester. Even the flexible nature of modular degrees can mean that some students experience a feeling of alienation. Other problems presented to counsellors include bereavement, pregnancy, substance abuse, family problems and eating disorders. '*The students who we will not see,*' says Anna, '*are "difficult" students who do not wish to see us. Tutors may sometimes feel, "this student needs a counsellor" but we quite firmly only see those who elect to see us. Nobody is sentenced to counselling here. It is never part of the disciplinary procedures.*'

Anna has noticed other changes in higher education counselling: '*We are certainly considered by the university as an essential part of the holistic educational experience,*' she says, and points out that the counselling team works closely with academic departments in the regular Quality Assurance exercises that contribute to the national university rankings. '*But,*' she continues, '*jobs are hard to get. Periodically we have to work in a climate of cuts. Currently my colleagues are employed "term-time only" or paid by the hour and on short-term contracts. A real full-time job with commensurate pay and conditions rarely comes up in London these days.*'

The aims of the BACP division for counsellors working in a university or college context include establishing student counselling as an integral part of the educational process. Anna's experience points up a number of issues that those working in the sector have to deal with, for example, counsellors in the sector have responsibilities not only to their primary client, the student, but also to themselves and to their institution.

Students are drawn from all sectors of society with many on part-time courses and many coming to education from outside the traditional routes. Counsellors working within the sector need a framework that will provide an understanding of and ability to deal with a variety of issues. A knowledge of adolescent development and the issues thrown up by the struggle for autonomy and the creation of a separate and defined space in the world underpins much of the work. This can also help in dealing with those mature students who find themselves thrown back into a situation that may reawaken adolescent strivings which they can find distressing. Additionally, as this case study shows, counsellors in higher education have to deal with the range of issues that crop up in any population of several thousand. This underlines the need for those wishing to work in the sector to get a thorough and continuing training.

Counsellors' responsibility to the employing institution may involve them running workshops and seminars for staff that serve to demystify counselling while at the same time disseminating their skills to others who are dealing with students. The counselling service can play an important role here and provide clear information to departments anxious about students who may be disturbed or disturbing yet who may not have any clear diagnosis of mental illness. The role of the counsellor in such situations can also bring up issues around confidentiality, and counsellors need clear guidelines to help them negotiate sometimes quite delicate boundary issues.

Another organisational issue, especially for counsellors in management roles, such as Anna, is the need to have a subtle grasp of the politics at work in the institution. This is particularly the case in situations where counselling services are endeavouring to have input to course and faculty review where they may not have a formal role.

The combination of the changing ethos, increased and conflicting demands holds potential dangers for counsellors in the sector. Consequently student counsellors are encouraged to continue their own personal and professional development to ensure that they attend to their own needs while they respond to the needs of others.

COUNSELLING IN THE WORKPLACE

Counsellors operating in this sector work with employees facing a wide range of issues. Many of these will be brought into the workplace from outside and problems at work can impact on employees' home life. Typical issues include:

- anxiety following the announcement of impending redundancies
- an employee displaying regular patterns of absence that may be associated with aspects of their job
- depression occuring several months after an employee has suffered a bereavement.

While there are different models for the provision of workplace counselling certain general principles apply. These include:

- the support of the organisation's senior management
- Management and supervisors' awareness of the service and individuals trained to enable them to identify employees with problems at an early stage
- the service needs to be accessible by all staff
- the emphasis should be on self-referral.

Counselling skills training is being taken up by managers and supervisors. This has helped counselling establish its value in the workplace but, at the same time, led to potential difficulties when these layers fail to recognise the appropriate point at which they should refer to the professional counsellor. A good counselling course, however, should be able to take this issue into account together with other important points such as confidentiality, record keeping and dealing with problems in open-plan offices.

In an ideal situation a professional counsellor will be seen as an ally by managers. Those working in this sector should be aware that they may face suspicion or hostility if the counsellors are perceived as a threat to disciplinary control or if managers feel that counsellors are encroaching on their areas. A counselling service will need to enrol support from managers, trade unions and employees. These groups will all bring their own perspective, which includes positive and negative elements.

CASE STUDY

Counselling in the workplace

Alan Rynn has been an employee counsellor with a local authority for ten years.

'When I answered the advert they were not asking for any qualifications, just appropriate experience. As an organisation today we still only ask for qualifications when they are required for a post. It is a sign of both the increased expectations of clients and the professional development of this sector of work that we now would ask for evidence of training that is in line with the BACP eligibility for counsellor accreditation.

'The organisation I work for provides much valuable support to employees through difficult events or phases of their lives, through its personnel, management and training. Over the years there has been an increasing recognition that some of the difficulties employees encounter may be helped by a counselling approach in which more time could be offered within a confidential framework for employees to address their concerns. Out of these aspirations has grown a dedicated counselling service.

'The employee base of the organisation is ethnically diverse and spans the age range of 16–65. The service is open to self-referral and management referrals. Employees present issues arising from their personal life such as relationship breakdown, changes in health status, bereavement, domestic violence, depression, anxiety and suicidal ideas. Work issues could involve workplace relationships, harassment, performance and absence, redundancy and ill-health retirement.

'Many employees make initial contact with the service when they feel in a crisis and feel they have come to the limit of their own and other's resources in trying to resolve their difficulties. Most employees using the service have not had prior experience of counselling. This means we have to clarify their perceptions about counselling and provide them with written and verbal information about the counselling relationship and the respective roles of counsellor and clients. This assists them in being clearer about what issues they want to address and they see the counsellor assisting them in that process.

'The service also sees employees who have been formally referred under Employer's Drug and Alcohol policy and those who have come through the encouragement of a manager. With both of these groups of prospective clients it is important to assess them and address the issue of choice in relation to seeing a counsellor and to see whether they can identify any benefits to themselves through attending further sessions. Without a personal commitment from an employee to address a situation further meetings could be fruitless for the employee and the counsellor and lead to the forming of a view by the employee that the counselling is an extension of the management system.

'As well as the core client work we also offer a consultancy service for managers around employee related matters. We are careful to differentiate this work from our client work as it recognises that managers are expected to respond to employee issues with reference to a range of employee-related policies. Often new managers and supervisors are developing their skills and competency through the experience of dealing with employee situations as they arise and may not have had to deal with something similar before. Managers bring a range of issues, which has included supporting staff after a workplace incident, exploring options for improving staff relations and addressing issues around alcohol misuse or performance issues.

'In addition to this the service runs workshops, training courses and sessions on other courses. For example, it has participated in the running of a twice yearly pre-retirement course, running sessions that focus on the change aspects that the new phase of life may have for employees as they relinquish a significant role in life and embark on developing other areas of fulfilment and interests. It has run workshops for managing bereavement in the workplace and training for supervisors on interviewing skills with employees.

'More recently the service ran a series of focus groups with employees to examine the sources of pressure in the workplace and the experience of stress arising from the workplace. The examples highlighted by employees were used as reference points in the shaping and delivery of a series of an organisational-wide stress management workshops to promote the employer's new stress management policy.

'Since I have been working here the whole employee counselling sector has become more organised and become clearer about its role and professionalism. I have been on a part-time counselling diploma course which I funded myself. Since I have been funded to do a two-year part-time certificate course in psychodynamic theory. While I generally work with clients in a person-centred way I have found that this course has really added something to my work. For example, an employee comes across some difficulties in asserting themselves in their relationships.

They introduce the issue about their dissatisfaction with the quality of the attention and the feedback they get from their supervisor during supervision. I would now consider whether this was an oblique reference to the counselling relationship and seek to clarify with the client whether there were issues concerning dissatisfactions they were feeling about my contributions.

'On the whole I would not advocate one counselling approach being more suitable than another for this kind of work. It seems to me that what is important centres on four elements. First, what is the client asking for help with in the assessment meeting, how do they think they can best be helped and do they may have a clear preference for a particular approach? Second, does the counselling approach offered fit in with the client's expectations of how they would like to be helped and is the focus of the work within the counsellor's competence? Third, is the client willing and able to enter a 'working relationship' with the counsellor. The fourth element is time. In common with many employee counselling services, sessions are limited. I currently work within a framework on an initial 'counselling needs' assessment session and up to eight further sessions. This is a short period of time. For some clients this may offer the opportunity to begin to orientate themselves in a period of crisis but will be insufficient for other clients to feel that they have begun to make real progress. The disruptive effect of entering into short-term counselling needs to be considered with the client, and other services more appropriate for them need to be identified.

'Within my own practice I have sought to incorporate aspects of different approaches that respond to the way in which a client wants to address their concern. For example, some individuals who have been involved in assaults or accidents want to focus on 'symptom reduction' and have a structured approach. This may include demonstrating relaxation and breathing techniques, focusing on rerunning the traumatic event, identifying with the client unhelpful messages contained within the talks they are having with themselves and helping them to develop more realistic appraisals of what has taken place. Other clients have wanted to unfold the experience in their own way and to focus on the meaning of the event for themselves and have preferred a more reflective and non-directive approach. The important thing is to get a thorough grounding in a particular approach, as this will provide the basis from which you can choose to incorporate other methods and techniques that you believe could be helpful to individual clients.

'This is definitely a growing area of counselling. Employers are becoming more aware of the effect of stress in the workplace and the implications it has for individuals and the organisation as a whole. I see an increasing number of adverts in the sector – many asking for BACP accreditation. We are large enough now to have our own sector, within BACP and there are regional associations which employee counselling services can join.'

LOOKING FOR WORK

Many of those completing diploma or advanced diploma courses will find they have already built up a kernel of clients. Some training institutions, such as the Westminster Pastoral Foundation, will have a graduate body that may also refer additional clients to you. Those who are looking for employment with an agency might consult publications and web sites operated by the accrediting bodies and publications such as the *New Statesman, Community Care, Times Educational Supplement, Times Higher Education Supplement* and *The Guardian*. Many of the sections of the BACP and organisations of the BACP, UKCP and the BCP will also have vacancy information for their members.

SALARIES

There are no national pay scales for counsellors. Even within the same sector such as higher education counsellors may be on different grades in different institutions. Full-time counselling posts may pay as little as £14,000 while higher paid posts may go up to £30,000. Those who take on additional management responsibilities with an organisation may earn up to £35,000. In private practice therapists need to charge enough to make a living while enrolling sufficient clients. Typically counsellors will charge between £30 and £40 per hour and psychotherapists between £35 and £45 per hour, though there are of course practioners who are able to charge considerably more than this.

Chapter 7
LIFE COACHING

Life coaches work with senior executives, entrepreneurs, students, people in career transition – anyone who needs help sorting out personal or professional problems. They help their clients formulate and achieve life goals, be it getting fitter, getting happier or getting richer. It originated in the USA but is growing rapidly in the UK. Currently there are around 450 life coaches working in the UK and a number of competing organisations offer training courses. Growth is being fuelled by the need for people to find balance in crowded lives and by the pressures of the contemporary economy.

Accurate figures for practitioners are hard to obtain because there is no central register and no single body authorised to offer quality assurance. This lack of regulation means that the life coaching movement is growing because of the reputations being built up by individual coaches with their clients rather than it being an established profession.

THE WORK OF LIFE COACHES

The fledgling UK market is developing many different niches, with coaches specialising in areas such as health, corporations, the arts, career transition and with the self-employed. Often these niches involve coaches using experience and skills they have acquired in previous careers. Coaching in the corporate sector is being conducted by more experienced practitioners and often has a focus on reorganisation and change management. Many firms operating in areas of skills shortages use the offer of life coaching to differentiate themselves from competitors, help them hold on to their most able staff and introduce a holistic staff development ethos. Corporate coaches may work with individuals – perhaps, for example, a new manager whose style conflicts with the company culture. Corporate life coaching is not the same as redundancy counselling but it may on occasion help individuals decide whether they are in the right company. Or coaches may work with groups on issues such as departmental communication problems, where they would typically meet with individuals before the group sessions to ensure they are tackling the core issues.

Most coaches also work with private clients covering a broad range of issues. This could involve helping clients experiencing chronic time management problems expressed through a disorganised desk, clients locked into overspending or people trying to find a balance between work commitments and other areas of their lives. Despite these issues life coaches are working with people who are reasonably well adjusted emotionally, often successful in their careers and business but who want more out of their lives. Life coaches do not try and replace other appropriate experts and regularly refer clients, for example to financial advisers and counsellors as part of the coaching practice.

COACHING AS A CAREER

Coaches are people who want to be inspirational and help 'make a difference'. They also find their work helps them with their own personal growth as problem solving with clients offers clues for their own lives. However, coaching is also growing because it offers an attractive way of earning a living – an hourly rate of £60 is not unusual. Most coaching is done by regular 30–45 minute telephone calls after a longer initial meeting and this means there is a lack of overheads and geographic flexibility. Having clients living or working in other countries is entirely possible.

TRAINING

Coaching does not claim to be counselling. It also differentiates itself from mentoring, training and therapy. Many coaches use a mixture of techniques with elements drawn from arenas as diverse as neuro-linguistic programming, personal development programmes and counselling. The unregulated nature of the movement means that coaches may be operating without any training. Indeed at least one training course actually *begins* with having its students 'declare themselves coaches'! Most coaches, however, will seek out training regularly to help them launch and sustain their work and to tap into a growing network of support and advice.

THE INTERNATIONAL COACHING FEDERATION

While there is no single 'approved' training course a number of courses have been validated by the International Coaching Federation (ICF). The ICF develops and promotes an industry-wide Code of Professional Standards and formats its accreditation process to 'preserve the integrity of coaching through internationally credible and ethical self-regulation'. The ICF is a non-profit, individual membership organisation formed by professionals worldwide who are involved with business and personal coaching. It offers several credentials for the coaching industry:

- **Certified Coach Training Agency (CCTA).** This recognises training organisations that are aligned with the ICF's definition of Professional Coaching, Standards and Code of Ethics.
- **Professional Certified Coach (PCC).** The ICF sees this as the first level of credential for a professional coach. Recognition at this level is via completion of a recognised course offered by a CCTA *plus* the accumulation of 750 coaching hours or $1\frac{1}{2}$ years work as a coach. Alternatively, following a 'portfolio' route coaches may accumulate 125 coaching-specific classroom hours in a range of coaching courses together with the 750 coaching hours and $1\frac{1}{2}$ years experience. This route also requires the successful completion of an ICF-administered exam.
- **Master Certified Coach (MCC).** This 'advanced' level of credential requires PCC plus evidence of successful completion of a minimum of 200 coaching-specific classroom hours, 2500 coaching hours or four years in the business of coaching. At this level coaches must also demonstrate leadership through visible contributions to the coaching profession.
- The ICF also offers the **Credentialing for Internal Corporate Coaches (CICC)** for individual coaches who are employed by and coaching within an organisation. This is not a significant feature of the UK coaching scene at present.

ICF requires coaches to become recertified every three years. This is relatively straightforward for those who are actively involved with coaching and requires evidence of significant further training through, for example, additional approved courses and break-out sessions from recognised conferences and workshops.

TRAINING ORGANISATIONS IN THE UK

The unregulated nature of the life coaching scene means that choosing an appropriate training course may not be straightforward. ICF accreditation is not essential to set up as a coach and in any case is only one criterion to take into account. Other factors to consider are:

- cost – most courses will cost several thousand pounds
- balance of individual and group work
- seminar versus telephone training
- balance of learners on the course – novices or experienced coaches
- length of training – courses may take around two years or three months, or even less; remember that longer courses may enable practitioners to reflect on and consolidate their experience.

There are growing numbers of organisations offering life coaching courses in the UK. These include the following.

The Coaches Training Institute

This American organisation offers ICF-approved training in the UK through partners Estrella Associates. Its distinctive 'Co-Active Coaching' model is delivered through a number of linked programmes. The foundation or level 1 'Co-Active Coaching Course' (CCC) takes 17 hours over three days in London, Bristol and Newcastle. Level 2 comprises four separate three-day courses – Fulfilment, Balance, Process and In the Bones. At 2001 prices CCC costs £390 and the four level 2 courses £490 each (all plus VAT). Beyond this and currently only available in the USA there is a 'mountain climb' of a programme to become a Certified Professional Co-active Coach (CPCC). This consists of a wide range of hands-on coaching, group instruction, supervision of coaching appointments, learning labs, required reading and a final exam.

There is currently only one CPCC coach in the UK, with several more completing certification soon.

For more information on the Coaches Training Institute contact Linda Taylor (UK), Estrella Associates Ltd; Tel: 01823 664441; e-mail: estrella.taylor@virgin.net; web site: www.thecoaches.com

CoachInc.com

CoachInc.com has pioneered the profession of coaching, training coaches in the USA since 1988. It now trains coaches in 43 countries worldwide.

About the programmes
CoachInc.com offers three complete coach training programmes: Coach Us Coach Training Programme (CTP); Corporate Coach Us, Corporate Business Coaching Programme (CBCP) and the Coaching Clinic Train the Trainer Programme. Corporate Coach Us also provides professionally trained coaches to the corporate marketplace.

Like most coaching in practice the training takes place over the telephone and includes: over 175 hours of in-depth coach training conducted by weekly conference calls called Tele-classes; comprehensive information and tools to help coaches work with clients; over 40 self-study workbooks and self-tests; guidance from a mentor coach; regular live coach skills workshops; access to teleconference bridges at cheap rates; an entry on CoachInc.com's web-based Coach Referral Service and membership of local groups; plus lifelong membership of CoachInc.com with access to free classes forever! The CTP programme costs approximately £2600 and the CBCP approximately £1800.

The Coaching Clinic Train the Trainer Programme is a training and licensing programme for individuals. The programme is ideal for external coaches, consultants and trainers who wish to have a tangible, sophisticated and highly developed product to take into the corporate marketplace, where they can train others to successfully use coaching skills to foster the rapid development of individuals and teams. The programme is also ideal for internal coaches who wish to increase their leadership effectiveness and/or train others in their organisations to become coaches.

Accreditation and certification

Both the CTP and CBCP programmes are ICF accredited and take about two years to complete. There is an additional certification programme for CoachInc.com graduates that equates to the ICF's PCC designation.

Experiencing CoachInc.com

A series of free weekly tele-classes are available for anyone with an interest in coaching or any of CoachInc.com's programmes. Also, live workshops are run regularly throughout the UK, giving participants the opportunity to find out more about the evolution of coaching as a profession and a chance to flex their coaching muscles.

For more information about any of CoachInc.com's programmes and forthcoming dates of virtual and live coaching skills experiences contact Carol Golcher; Tel: 0800 0854317; e-mail: carol@coachu.com, web site: www.coachinc.com.

The Life Coaching Academy

While not currently accredited by the ICF the Life Coaching Academy (LCA) is well known in coaching circles and was one of the earliest organisations offering training in the UK. It is now the largest provider in Europe and second largest in the world. Training starts with a residential two-day workshop that includes themed sessions with opportunities to practise coaching. During the workshop participants learn things such as:

- what it means to be a life coach – obligations, commitments and responsibilities
- a coaching model – a structure that allows you to coach effectively and successfully
- the first coaching session – what to say and do during the first session to ensure the client's progress
- practical sessions – a chance to practise what has been learnt and get constructive feedback on your performance
- how to market yourself and find clients – essential if you plan to start your own practice.

Following the residential workshop students are appointed their own mentor coach who offers guidance through a distance-learning course of workbooks and offers practical, experience-based feedback on your coaching skills and development. Students are encouraged to join a 'coaching circle' – informal monthly meetings of coaches throughout the UK. A distinctive feature of the LCA course is a fortnightly live coaching call. These are 'conference calls' themed around different areas of coaching. Participation in these calls is included in your course fee, for just the cost of the phone call.

Graduation from LCA follows after completion of six of the above calls, plus a written critique on a book chosen from an approved reading list, a thesis and successful completion of an assessment paper designed to probe your coaching philosophy. These are assessed and marked independently by experienced, hand-picked assessors of the LCA.

There are further opportunities for additional study and, with increased experience, LCA graduates can apply for Senior or Fellow status with the Academy.

The standard LCA course fee is £2495 including VAT (including all meals and accommodation on the residential workshop). Further information from web site: www.lifecoachingacademy.com, Tel: 0800 783 4823; e-mail: info@lifecoachingacademy.com.

CASE STUDY

Penni Blythe – life coach

Penni's business, Centre for Creative Change, is based in Somerset but has corporate and individual clients all over the UK. Her education and training consultancy business has been built up over a number of years but the incorporation of life coaching into her practice over the last 13 months has resulted in a number of changes – a new business orientation and a subtle new logo amongst them: 'The logo was created for me by a top-class designer as barter for some life coaching', says Penni. 'It needed to be different and dynamic enough for the corporate market as well as appealing to individuals.' More fundamentally life coaching has reoriented Penni's business:

'I now choose different work. I recently turned down a project evaluating a curriculum, "toolkit" – it seemed mechanistic to me. I now look more for work where the clients are wanting change. But it also means I work differently with those clients I do work with, for example I have recently facilitated a strategic planning day with a voluntary arts group. Because of my life coaching I was less concerned with the "action bits" and much more with helping the group get their shared vision clear. They are now in a better position to organise relevant actions. Before life coaching it would have been more about "doing" and less about "exploring".'

Penni's consultancy has been founded on her considerable experience in the education, training and development field. '*After university I trained as a teacher but even then I knew my interests lay in a more developmental approach to education.*' Penni returned to teaching in her thirties after working in a research role in a corporate headquarters and even had a spell as a computer programmer. '*I wasn't a very good programmer but it taught me a lot. I knew I wanted to teach if I could find a role that could take account of what I had done.*' Penni taught and managed in the further education sector before becoming involved with staff and curriculum development on a regional basis. Then, after a brief spell organising and delivering educational training conferences, she was confronted with a life choice – '*being true to myself or following what was there. So I took a risk and went freelance.*' Her clients were colleges, voluntary groups, businesses and quangos:

'Even before life coaching I was finding myself working with people to realise their dreams. A college delivering an ambitious curriculum within a specific financial model, for example; a voluntary group of folk music enthusiasts who wanted to gain funding to set up a folk development organisation or a company wanting to design effective management skills in senior and middle management staff. Then along came life coaching.

'A colleague recommended the Co-Active Coaching book to me and I quickly got myself on an introductory course. I have been working since I was 13 years old and been in development work since I was 21. I am a great "explorer" but I am also really critical when it comes to training but I was really impressed by the quality of the training on the course. I was struck by their integrity, creativity and their ability to get straight to the point.' I've always wanted to make a difference. Even as a teacher it was never about "my subject". It was always about helping people finding their passion.'

Penni quickly took more advanced courses with CTI and began turning individual 'practice' clients into paying clients after a couple of sessions. '*My first client insisted on paying after a couple of practice sessions because he was getting so much out of it,*' says Penni. '*I was shocked, amazed and thought "Wow!" but the transition to a fee basis seemed quite natural.*'

Penni's clients form a continuum, with individual clients at one end through small groups and whole companies at the other. She clearly loves her mission – '*empowering people to live their dreams.*' Recently, for example, she has been working on supporting transition with 14–19 year olds. This comes 20 years after first working with young people as a teacher. Thanks to life coaching though, it clearly feels not so much 'full circle' as working at a higher point on a spiral.

COACHING AND COUNSELLING DISTINCTIONS

Coaching does not claim to be counselling but it is not opposed to counselling. Many life coaches are also trained counsellors and there are many common elements in the work. These include the existence of a one-to-one, confidential relationship; the fact that clients in both coaching and therapy want change; and the common assumption that change will come over a period of time. Key differences however, focus on the content of the sessions, the context of the relationship and the condition of the client.

Coaching	Therapy
PARADIGMS/MODELS	
Sports training/coaching Personal growth seminars	Medicine and healing
WORKS WITH PEOPLE WHO ARE	
Asking how-to questions Designing their future, learning new skills	Asking 'why' questions Dealing with rooted issues, emotional pain, or traumas
APPROACH	
Primary focus on actions and the future Assist clients in identifying, prioritising and implementing choice Directs the client to return to action	Focus on feelings and history Assists clients in untangling unconscious conflicts which interfere with choice Directs the client to go deeper into feelings
PROCESS	
Focus on learning and developing potential Deals mainly with external issues; looks for external solutions to internal blocks	Focus on healing and restoring function Deals mainly with internal issues; looks for internal resolution

Chapter 8
FURTHER INFORMATION

ADDRESSES

British Association for Counselling and Psychotherapy, 1 Regent Place, Rugby, Warwickshire CV21 2JP
Tel: 0870 4435170; Minicom: 0870 4435162; web site: www.counselling.co.uk

British Confederation of Psychotherapists, 37 Mapesbury Road, London NW2 4HJ
Tel: 020 8452 9823; e-mail: mail@bcp.org.uk; web site: www.bcp.org.uk

COSCA (formerly the Confederation of Scottish Counselling Agencies), 18 Viewfield Street, Stirling FK8 2BX
Tel: 01786 475 140; enquiries@cosca.org.uk; web site: www.cosca.org.uk

The British Psychological Society, St Andrew's House, 48 Princess Road East, Leicester LE1 7DR
Tel: 0116 254 9568; e-mail: enquiry@bps.org.uk; web site: www.bps.org.uk

United Kingdom Council for Psychotherapy, 167–169 Great Portland Street, London W1W 5PF
Tel: 020 7436 3002; E-mail: admin@ita.org.uk; ukcp@psychotherapy.org.uk; website: www.psychotherapy.org.uk

VOLUNTEERING

National Centre for Volunteering, Regents Wharf, 8 All Saints Street, London N1 9RL
Tel: 020 7520 8900; web site www.volunteering.org.uk (includes links to partner bodies in Scotland, Wales and Northern Ireland)

Relate, Herbert Gray College, Little Church Street, Rugby CV21 3AP
E-mail: field-services@national.relate.org.uk; web site: www.relate.org.uk

PUBLICATIONS

Co-Active Coaching, Laura Whitworth, Henry Kimsey-House and Phil Sandahl, Davies-Black.

Counselling in Action Series, Series Editor Windy Dryden, Sage.

Counselling as a Career, Robert Ross, Baldrick Press.

First Steps in Counselling, Pete Sanders, PCCS Books.

Handbook of Counselling, edited by Stephen Palmer/associate editor Gladea McMahon, Routledge.

Handbook of Individual Therapy, edited by Windy Dryden, Sage.

Is Counselling Training For You?, Val Potter, Insight.

Training in Counselling and Psychotherapy Directory, BACP.